BARBARA ERNST PREY

NOCTURNES

*Meditations on the
Environment*

Nocturnes: Barbara Ernst Prey

Printed in China by C & C Offset Printing, Inc.
ISBN-13 978-1-60643-515-1

Sarah Cash is the Bechhoefer Curator of American Art at the Corcoran Gallery of Art in Washington, D.C.

www.barbaraprey.com

Cover: *Nocturne*, 2008, watercolor on paper, 21 x 28 inches

TABLE OF CONTENTS

Nocturnes: Meditations on the Environment by Barbara Ernst Prey

This essay by Sarah Cash, Bechhoefer Curator of American Art at The Corcoran Gallery of Art, is reproduced from the recent exhibition catalogue accompanying the exhibit *Barbara Ernst Prey: An American View* on view from October 17, 2007 - January 13, 2008 at The Mona Bismarck Foundation, Paris, France. The exhibit was also co-curated by Sarah Cash.

Barbara Ernst Prey: An American View

In early February 2007 I taught a short art history course to a group of museum-going adults who, during my preparations, were described to me as "lifelong learners." Scarcely a week later, Barbara Ernst Prey and I contemplated her life and work in the bright warmth of her Long Island home and studio (fig. 1). It then occurred to me that the painter, perhaps more than anyone I have ever known, personifies that vernacular in her enthusiastic, seemingly insatiable embrace of the myriad learning opportunities offered by life, particularly a life in art. She has made art with intense energy and deep commitment since her childhood, and continues to do so at every juncture, whether working in her studio or seeking out new painting sites. In pursuit of her goals,

fig. 1

moreover, she eagerly espouses new ideas, views, and viewpoints, whether or not related to her art-making. In short, she possesses (and exhibits) a heartfelt passion for life, art, and their inherent and always provocative interconnectedness.

Embodying this curiosity and fervor is the artist's credo: "always ask why." Underlying her consideration of landscape subjects for their aesthetic merit is Prey's investigation of her surroundings on deeper levels that are at once emotional and intellectual. Throughout her career, she has examined communities inhabited by people whose lives and traditions most connect with the land and the sea. The resulting paintings, while stylistic and technical *tours de force*, also express her concern for humankind's relationship to our fragile natural world. This probing beneath, behind,

5

and around the structures and views that she paints—her avid search for the "why" in environments as diverse as the historic Taiwanese city of Tainan, rural Pennsylvania, suburban Long Island, and coastal Maine—has its roots in her unusual background.

A strong academic footing in studio art and the histories of art, architecture, and theology; disciplined field and studio practice characterized by intense and exacting study of subject, color, and light; and a rich accumulation of diverse life experiences have shaped Prey's development as an artist, as well as her devotion to always asking why. That background, combined with her skilled eye and her appetite for knowledge and aesthetic beauty, yield Prey's American view. Hers is a view describing the built and natural environments of her unseen human subjects: landscapes, seascapes, places of worship, farmhouses, fishing boats, buoy workshops, pumpkins, quilts, American flags, and more. In many instances, moreover, the artist infuses her views with sometimes subtle, sometimes overt messages of uniquely American events and stories: the increasingly difficult lives of Maine lobster fishermen; the profound tragedy of September 11, 2001; the chilly loneliness of poor rural America.

A childhood of artistic ferment

Prey's aesthetic sensibilities took root during a youth surrounded by art. She often cites the profound and lasting influence of her artist mother, Peggy Ernst (née Margaret Louise Joubert, 1923-2005), (fig. 2),

fig. 2

who taught design for nine years at New York City's Pratt Institute, one of the country's oldest and most distinguished colleges of art and design.[1] Mother and daughter spent time together painting and drawing—"I always drew," remarks Prey—in and around the family home in Manhasset, Long Island, and on occasional painting trips nearby. They painted oil and watercolor still lifes arranged by Peggy in her studio, as well as landscapes in the wooded backyard. Foretelling her later development as a painter of coastal scenes, as a teenager Prey painted watercolors of ocean views while perched on the rocky shore of nearby Long Island Sound. The Sound was visible from her mother's studio, just as it is from Barbara's light-filled, third-floor workspace in Oyster Bay.

Peggy Ernst's oils and watercolors—made close to home and on travels to picturesque locales such as Key West, Bermuda, the Bahamas, Jamaica, and Hawaii—and her many art books were omnipresent in the Ernst home for her daughter's interest and enjoyment. Also important for Barbara's future was her mother's display of reproductions of Winslow Homer's (1836-1910) watercolors depicting the brilliant landscapes and seascapes of Key West and Bermuda. These undoubtedly were acquisitions inspired by Peggy's trips, later purchased during periodic mother-daughter trips to art museums in nearby New York City.[2] Less conventional was Peggy's attempt to adjust the view from her home's terrace by covering a grey birch tree with white paint, reminiscent of Frederic Church's realignment of the landscape elements around his Hudson River mansion to achieve his desired sight lines.[3]

This mother-daughter artistic camaraderie fed Prey's avid and active interest in making art; she contributed a watercolor to her first juried adult show at age twelve. Soon afterward, as a teenager, she began to paint watercolors in earnest, including several serene still lifes forecasting her love of saturated color. Inspiring and supportive teachers in grade school and, later, high school nurtured her talent; her strong draughtsmanship is evident in an animated study of a tree. Visits to New York City museums provided the inspiration for two high school projects. In one, a large-scale acrylic mural, Prey looked to several works by Henri Rousseau as muses, including *La Rêve* (1910, Museum of Modern Art). Another project was a large painting of a block of buildings in Manhasset's downtown, inspired by Edward Hopper's *Early Sunday Morning* (1930, Whitney Museum of American Art); although unlocated, the canvas is well-represented by the artist's evocative, light-filled study. Remarkably, in the midst of all of this artistic activity and ferment, the precocious student spent the summer before her senior year in high school at the San Francisco Art Institute.

"Not just to look, but also to see"

Prey's artistic development continued in full force as she entered Williams College, her aesthetic vision nurtured by the school's picturesque setting in Massachusetts' Berkshire Mountains. There she continued her study of studio art and received her first exposure to the history of art under the tutelage of some of the finest faculty in the world, with access to the world-renowned collections of the Williams College Museum of Art and the Sterling and Francine Clark Art Institute.[4] She was now able to study firsthand the oils and watercolors of

7

Winslow Homer and Edward Hopper, works that were to exert a lasting influence on her work. Hungry for as much exposure to original works of art as her schedule allowed, she worked as a museum monitor at Williams and as a docent at the Clark. During her junior year study in Munich and travels in Europe, she continued to look and sketch; during this time she made a first trip to Paris, where she visited the Louvre, Musée D'Orsay, and the Musée de Cluny. Never idle, following her senior year at Williams, she supplemented an internship at New York's Metropolitan Museum of Art with frequent study of the treasures in the nearby Frick Collection.

The remarkable amount of art and architecture Prey absorbed in four years spent in Williamstown, New York, and in Europe is indelibly etched in her razor-sharp memory. These works continue to serve as her muses, and she often speaks passionately and knowledgeably about her encounters with them: Medieval manuscripts in a class with the venerable historian of French art and architecture Whitney Stoddard; the line and color of stained glass at Chartres and the Musée de Cluny; French and German ecclesiastical architecture and sculpture in lectures and on-site at Vezelay and Chartres; and an exhibition of Mogul paintings at the Clark Art Institute. Prey peppers discussions of her work with references to numerous and varied inspirations in the Clark's collection, ranging from the color in early Netherlandish painting to that in Paul Gauguin's work, and from Albrecht Dürer's line to John Singer Sargent's bravura handling of white-on-white.

It was also during this period that Prey developed a pivotal and lifelong friendship with the late art historian S. Lane Faison, Jr., legendary teacher and mentor to generations of Williams-educated artists, art historians, and art lovers.[5] It was Faison's emphasis on the connection between art and history that so strongly informed the artist's "always ask why" principle, her melding of disciplines that sets her apart from many other artists: he exhorted her (and likely many others) "not just to look, but also to see" according to Prey. Similarly, in his teaching, Faison, emphasized the importance of understanding "the connection of art to history," particularly that "every work of art was done somewhere and some when...".[6] As Prey herself states: "I am always looking, looking, looking....The skills you learn in art history translate to painting as an artist. You are a creator, an observer, and an interpreter, distilling your subject. Drawing on my extensive opportunities to study art around the world, [when I paint] I incorporate what I like and dismiss what doesn't apply."

Beyond the ivory tower: travels and more looking

Following Williams, Prey returned to southern Germany on a Fulbright scholarship, where she remained for two years, spending much of her time absorbing that country's rich cultural heritage. Besides cultivating her continuing interest in northern European architecture and sculpture, the artist looked intently at painters such as the nineteenth-century German Romantic painter Caspar David Friedrich, particularly the twilight and snow subjects. These works served as a springboard for Prey's works such as *Twilight* and *Twilight II*, and would later resonate with her interest in the nineteenth-century marine painter Fitz Henry Lane and other American painters associated with the Hudson River School.

Returning to the U.S. in 1981, Prey was exposed to numerous works by Henri Matisse and other artists of the School of Paris as a cataloguer in the modern painting department at Sotheby's auction house in New York City. It was also at this time that she began to focus intently on drawing and to sell her work to important publications such as the *New Yorker*, which bought and reproduced her illustrations for over ten years. Magazines such as *Gourmet, Good Housekeeping,* and *Horticulture,* as well as the venerable *New York Times,* followed suit, granting wide exposure to Prey's lyrical sketches of architecture, genre, and still-life subjects. As she acknowledges, her earlier study of the lines of late-Gothic German sculpture, woodcuts, and etchings, as well as the woodcuts of the early Renaissance master Albrecht Dürer, was important for these drawings. The work of another *New Yorker* artist, French cartoonist Jean-Jacques Sempé, also inspired this body of work, as did the fluid draughtsmanship of Matisse and of Jean-Auguste-Dominique Ingres.[7]

Prey continued her illustration work when she entered Harvard Divinity School in 1984, where she was inspired to pursue her Master's degree as a result of her years of exposure to Medieval, Romanesque, and Baroque art and architecture. At Harvard she probed more deeply into the ecclesiastical history that inspired the design and execution of those monuments. She also furthered her study of art history to include the art and religion of ancient Greece and Renaissance Rome, as well as Chinese landscape painting, while still sharpening her eye by frequently visiting Harvard's Fogg and Busch-Reisinger museums. Significantly, despite her intellectual activity in urban Cambridge, Prey's personal sensibilities and her art-making remained closely allied with the land and the sea. She made her home in the rural towns of Boston's picturesque north shore, where she continued to draw and paint.

Abroad again: 1986-1987

Soon after her graduation from Harvard, for the first time, Prey was able to steadily manifest in her art her intense study of buildings and objects, their adornments and surroundings, and the people and functions for which they were designed. This opportunity came in the form of a Henry Luce Foundation grant to work and travel in Tainan, Taiwan, and throughout Asia. In those locales, Prey continued to learn new

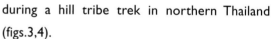

fig. 3

artistic styles and techniques by studying with a Chinese Master Painter. She also delved deeply into the lives and inspirations of her subjects by researching Chinese folk religion, noting:

> When I paint, I distill my surroundings. In the Taiwan paintings, for example, I was observing what inspires people, how they live their lives. The temples were interesting structures in and of themselves, but also embodied the Taiwanese' strong religious beliefs, a mixture of Confucianism, Buddhism, and Animism.

This first full coalescing of the artist's background, interests, and inspirations bore important fruit. During her first year in Tainan, Prey's progress and confidence inspired her to move beyond her intimately-scaled watercolors. Her first large, full-sheet paintings were the highly detailed *Confucius Temple* and the poignant *East Looks West*, the latter a masterful study in light and silhouette. In developing her signature format, Prey was at once the observer and the observed. An anomaly both in appearance and pastime, she fascinated her new acquaintances, whether in an urban Tainan neighborhood or during a hill tribe trek in northern Thailand (figs.3,4).

From China to Appalachia, 1988-1996

In 1988 Prey relocated to western Pennsylvania with her husband Jeffrey, trading the rich social, cultural, and religious traditions of Asia for those of a vastly different environment. In the small Appalachian town of Prosperity, the artist revived the "research and immersion" methodology she had developed in Taiwan. She spent considerable time getting to know the buildings, local traditions, and hilly landscape vistas of that rural area as well as its residents, whose livelihoods ranged from farming to factory work to coal mining.

One of the many rich folk traditions of Appalachia is quilting, an activity that fosters community amongst the women and families of this historically isolated area. As succinctly stated by one quilting organization: "Quilts tell stories; they illustrate history; they express love and sorrow; they link generations together; they are community; people gather to make them and experience them; they are art;

fig. 4

they teach."[8] Having learned of their importance to her neighbors and the local community, Prey chose quilts as the subject of one of her most accomplished watercolors developed during this period, *Americana*. The colorful, detailed patchwork quilts, their fluttering surfaces so masterfully captured, might at first glance seem a departure in subject matter from Prey's earlier architectural and landscape views. However, just as those European and Asian subjects are symbolic of their creators, the quilts are emblematic of the proud and industrious Appalachian people and their unique culture.

Of all of Prey's work, *Americana* has perhaps the most personal meaning for the artist. The quilts depicted were made by members of the Preys' church, who gave the right-hand one to the family as a gift of friendship

A Return to Roots: Long Island and Maine

In 1996, the Preys relocated again, to Oyster Bay, Long Island. In many 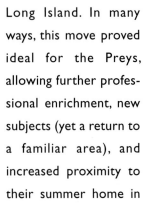 ways, this move proved ideal for the Preys, allowing further professional enrichment, new subjects (yet a return to a familiar area), and increased proximity to their summer home in Port Clyde, Maine, on the St. George Peninsula. It is Maine, where Prey has been painting since she first visited as a college student, that has engendered the most artistic continuity—as well as the most growth and change—in the artist's work. The pull of historic mid-coast Maine, including its residents and traditions, has been strong for her, just as it has been for generations of American artists.[9] Moreover, it is not only Maine's history as a landscape subject to which Prey feels a keen emotional connection; she has family roots on the St. George Peninsula dating to the 1700s, when her mother's ancestors lived in some of the same white houses that she has taken as her subjects.

Prey's work from her thirty years in Maine, her best-known and most mature, has taken to a new level her singular ability to observe, study, and capture the unique characteristics of her environment. Watercolors like *Americana*, developed in Pennsylvania, transformed into a series of paintings featuring Maine quilts, such as *Reunion* and *Reunion at Dusk* and *After the Rain*. While quilting is a folk tradition shared by the residents of (among other places) rural Pennsylvania and Maine, Prey has sought out the unique aspects of life on the Maine coast. The area's hard-working inhabitants, whose daily lives and surroundings are steeped in seafaring and lobstering traditions, capture the artist's eye year after year. She has created light-filled compositions detailing elements of the lives, work, and habitat of the lobster fishermen who are her neighbors during the summer months. It is a powerful sense of human presence—despite the absence of the figure—infused with a compelling aura of place and history that, above all, characterizes this group of Prey's exquisitely conceived and rendered watercolors.

The artist's sharply observed, painstakingly rendered portrayals explore the built environ-

ments most important to the lobster fishermen—their homes, boats, and buoy-filled winter workshops—all situated in the context of their natural surroundings of land and sea. The carefully detailed, majestic *The Apple House*, for example, is not only inhabited by one of the artist's seafaring neighbors, but also surely has housed fishermen throughout the centuries of its existence. Its traditional New England architectural form of connected farm buildings, the so-called "big house, little house, back house, barn," still so ubiquitous in rural Maine, is an institution in and of itself.

As the artist has noted, these structures connect their inhabitants and us, as viewers, to the land (and the sea); these scenes link us to place, history, and elemental human pursuits in the face of our frenetic, technology-dominated lives. "The architecture," she muses, "tells a story of Maine." By extension, the fisherman's boats and buoys—the other "structures" in her work—also play important roles in telling the story of the state's coastal inhabitants and their traditions. *The Simple Life*, whose proud subject, stark composition, and crisp handling betray its title, is—both cause of and in spite of its evident straightforwardness—emblematic of that story. (The same might be said of that painting's nautical equivalent, *Wayfarers*). It is the successful realization of her desire to connect her images to history, tradition, and the land that aligns Prey with earlier American painters whose work has influenced her own.

Prey's pristine Maine landscapes and seascapes evoke the power and permanence of nature in contrast to the comparative insignificance and transience of human life, a belief held dear by the Hudson River School painters of a century and a half ago. *The Long Haul*, for example, calls to mind the sensibilities of Fitz Henry Lane's tranquil harbor scenes such as *Shipping in Down East Waters* (c. 1850, The Farnsworth Art Museum).[10] It does so not only in subject and masterful handling of atmospheric effects and reflections, but also in the suggestion of the enduring presence of nature and its spiritual associations. The simple, gray lobsterman's workshop in the middle ground of *Birdhouses* set on the edge of a sweeping meadow detailed with the subtle greens and browns of fall grasses, recalls the diminutive mountain cabin seen in some of Thomas Cole's landscapes that symbolized the ultimate inadequacy of man relative to God's presence in nature.[11] The artist also shares the American Impressionist painters' exultant yet historically suggestive approach to their themes. Quite often these were views in the New England landscape, "rich not only in historical associations but also in personal significance…subjects that enabled [the American Impressionists] to express ideas and sentiments that appealed to an audience that cherished tradition and continuity in the face of change."[12]

The changes facing turn-of-the-twentieth-century Americans primarily involved increasing immigration and urbanization. Those faced by the U.S. one hundred years later are vastly more complex, ranging from the environment to rapidly changing technology to national security. Like her predecessors, Prey is keenly aware that modern events as well as historical patterns hold powerful sway over the way we experience our surroundings. And like many of her artist contemporaries, she struggled with questions of her work's relevance after the tragedies of September 11, 2001. In rural Maine, she observed and recorded the sudden ubiquity of American flags, clustered on a front porch here, tied to a church railing there—locating in an historical moment the otherwise timeless weathered clapboard architecture that had long served among her subjects. Less overt tributes to the Twin Towers are embedded in a painting whose sole focus is a pair of windows; one shades an American flag, and both are touched by graceful climbing roses as if in peaceful memoriam.

13

In addition to broader national issues, Maine's particular twenty-first-century changes are the opposite of those faced by turn-of-the-twentieth-century Americans. Rather than flocking to the cities to pursue work and the "American dream" in increasingly developed surroundings, many post-September 11 Americans are retreating to Maine and other rural environs seeking a simpler lifestyle. The irony of this influx of people "from away," of course, is that the resulting increase in property values and real estate development in Maine imperils precisely that which is so eagerly sought: the pristine and history-laden character of the landscape and the traditional *modus vivendi* nurtured by it.[13] In turn, this reversal will seriously challenge the "tradition and continuity" treasured by the longtime Maine residents whose lives and livelihoods are the subjects of Prey's paintings. Ironically, these very ideals may also be endangered by the lobster industry itself. While Port Clyde ranked among New England's major fishing ports for the first time in 2003, that same year the western part of Penobscot Bay elected to reduce the number of lobstermen in this lucrative area (which encompasses Port Clyde). Some fishermen fear that this resolution will jeopardize their younger compatriots and those inhabiting smaller islands and towns, as well as the operators of smaller boats.[14] As the artist muses, "I am chronicling a way of life that may not always be."

In these works the sense of place and its history, both natural and human, is intensified and universalized through the absence of the figure. Prey contends that a figure or figures would "stop the viewer" and assume the focus of attention, becoming the provider of a bounded narrative. Instead, the viewer's response to her watercolors is open-ended. The renderings of landscape, seascape, structures, and boats may be valued either for their considerable aesthetic appeal and technical mastery (belying the often difficult lives of their occupants), or for their evocation of something deeper, more spiritual or personal; we often yearn to know more about the lives of these families. In this way, the works find their closest parallel in the paintings and watercolors of Edward Hopper, who, according to his fellow painter Guy Pène du Bois, "never stopped…preferring to portray houses and steam engines to men."[15] His paintings of Maine and Cape Cod farmhouses, boats, and landscapes share with works such as *Early Risers* a weighted, nearly mystical character and the invitation to imagine human presence, rendered in an unaffected representational style.[16] The painter Charles Burchfield's eloquent analysis of Hopper's approach resonates when considering Prey's views:

Hopper's viewpoint is essentially classic; he presents his subjects without sentiment, or propaganda, or theatrics. He is the pure painter, interested in his material for its own sake, and in the exploitation of his idea of form, color, and space division. In spite of his restraint, however, he achieves such a complete verity that you can read into his interpretations of houses...any human implications you wish; and in his landscapes there is an old primeval Earth feeling that bespeaks a strong emotion felt, even if held in abeyance.[17]

fig. 5

The absence of evident navigators in *Optimist* or of laborers in *Work in Progress*, then, allow the viewer to contemplate the seafarers' hopes, dreams, and livelihood, and thereby to sense their presence, their activity, and the spaces they occupy. While there is no comparison between the ultimate, unseen meaning of these images and the tragic space shuttle disaster memorialized in *Columbia Tribute*, the artist's observation on her choice of subject for the latter commission resonates with her carefully chosen Maine themes.

She has stated that she wanted to capture the spirit of the astronauts by portraying the vessel that embodied their hopes and dreams, the marker of a place and of an activity so important in the lives of its unseen protagonists.[18] Besides the Columbia painting, her distinguished NASA commissions include those for paintings of the International Space Station (2003), the x-43 (2005), and the Shuttle Discovery's return to flight (2005, fig.5). Perhaps not surprisingly, the artist notes that these projects have helped her realize the fragility of the world and man's place in it. Commenting on her intense dedication to researching every subject and its underlying essence, she notes: "Just as I researched Chinese religion when painting the temples of Tainan, I spent eighteen months studying my NASA subjects in order to complete my commissions."

In the Maine works, our imaginations are enticed not only by the houses, boats, and sheds themselves, but also by the exquisitely wrought details that animate the compositions: the particular shape of a hull that bespeaks a boat's place of origin, the vibrant paint colors chosen by the fisherman to distinguish their trap buoys. One wonders about the resolute women, living or dead, who painstakingly sewed the quilts drying on clotheslines in *Early Risers*; the personality who inscribed his favorite beer brand on the rafters of his workshop; or the family member who so sensitively arranged starfish on a window sash above a blooming geranium, just as sensitively rendered by the artist with a hint of *japonisme* in the delicate apple tree limbs that complete the composition *Harvest* and *Branch Hangers*.

These details are nowhere more densely

fig. 6

worked or meticulously rendered than in the group of winter workshop interiors, the most innovative compositions in this series and an entirely new subject for Prey. Inspired in part by the highly decorated interior depicted on the 2003 White House Christmas card (fig.6),—another highly prestigious U.S. Government commission that the artist carefully researched and executed —these intricately composed works also testify to her predilection for strong color and her interest in probing beneath exterior appearances. "I've always been fascinated with what is inside, from the outside looking in," the artist admits, voicing the innocently voyeuristic pastime pursued by many. Two ambitious watercolors in the 2004 sub-series, for example, *Bait House* and *Blue Note*, provide glimpses into these bright and congenial havens for the off-season work of trap repair, buoy painting, and line cleaning, as well as socializing.[19] The tiers upon tiers of painstakingly drawn and painted buoys—still lifes, as the artist notes—provide a stark contrast to the windows betraying the cold, foggy coastline beyond. Together, these elements comprise a perfect case study of Prey's mastery of the unforgiving medium of watercolor (seen to completely different, but just as compelling, effect in the masterful *Ghost House*). Since not a single element may be changed after it has been painted, the artist prepares methodically for the final compositions. Repeated visits to steal glimpses of these workshops yielded photographs for study and, later, luminous sketches carefully squared off for eventual enlargement. This working method is also seen to instructive effect by comparing the intimately-scaled *Evening Palette, Study*, to the finished work *Evening Palette*. Differences in palette, composition, and handling of the sky reveal the thoughtful, meticulous process in which the artist engages as she progresses to her finished paintings.

Like the lobster fisherman's hardscrabble, tradition-laden work so easily overlooked by the tourist who sees only the romanticism of the seafaring life (or the price per pound), the rigors and complexities of Prey's own work may, to some, be eclipsed by the peacefulness of her images. Pure form and hue are here judged on their own considerable merits, but the viewer is simultaneously challenged to question existing assumptions about the appearance of watercolor; these are, after all, more paintings than works on paper in their edge-to-edge color and in their many layers of wash, allowing alternating passages of translucency and opacity. Moreover, we are provoked to think more deeply about their subject matter, to imagine beyond the vessels and buildings, venturing in our mind's eye deep into the lives and spirits of their unseen occupants, into the story of Maine.

Barbara Ernst Prey's career is thirty-five years young; her lifelong learning continues unabated. "We look and we learn and we incorporate and then we put our own mark, world view, and experience in to the work," muses Prey. The artist continues to take the watercolor medium, which has an august role in the history of American art, to innovative—yet traditionally rooted—places. Looking as well as seeing, she searches out new vistas, compositions, and ideas in the landscapes and environments that are her home. Recently, some of her work has exhibited more abstract tendencies. There are lone, large-scale boats set against stark backgrounds of deep blue water, not bounded by foreground or sky; buoy workshops whose exteriors read like color field paintings; and minimal, nearly abstract seascapes devoid of the familiar boats. Lone figures enliven more narrative works, yet those images share with the other recent paintings a minimal sensibility and nearly mystical feeling. In still another group, the artist examines familiar surroundings during different weather effects or times of day such as *Twilight* and *First Snowfall*.

Perhaps Prey's observations on her choice of watercolor as a medium serve as the consummate metaphor for her ongoing development and experimentation as a painter. She remarks on the deep appeal of the technique's fluidity while recognizing its simultaneously unpredictable nature, which often necessitates improvisation. Watercolor, she notes, "develops on its own…you have an idea, but the beauty is in the process."

Sarah Cash,
May 2007

Author's Note: The author would like to express sincere thanks to Barbara Ernst Prey for her patience and assistance with the preparation of this essay. Unless otherwise indicated, any quotes from, or paraphrasing of, Barbara Ernst Prey derive from in-person and telephone interviews conducted with the artist between January 2005 and May 2007, as well as e-mails received from her during that time. This research was conducted both in preparation for the 2007/2008 exhibition at The Mona Bismarck Foundation and accompanying publication as well as for the 2005 exhibition and catalogue of Prey's work entitled *Works on Water* (see bibliography). Some of the text in the current essay addressing Prey's Maine work derives from the author's essay in the *Works on Water* catalogue.

[1] Prey's relentless pursuit of her art-making resonates with the fact that her mother declined Pratt's offer to become its first dean of women in order to continue teaching. She served as instructor in two-dimensional design at Pratt from 1947-1956 (email to the author from Paul Schlotthauer, Pratt Librarian and Archivist, May 8, 2007). Prey cites her father, Herbert Ernst (1898-1985), as always supportive of her mother, herself, and their careers; he also helped to inspire his daughter's love of nature. A successful professional orthodontist (and Columbia University faculty member) whose New York City practice attracted prominent international clients, Ernst was an educated, cultured, and worldly figure whose love of music, travel, and above all, knowledge, strongly influenced Prey's life and work.

[2] The Homer watercolor reproductions included *Nassau* and *Flower Garden and Bungalow, Bermuda* (both 1899, Metropolitan Museum of Art). These prints were complemented by one reproducing Homer's oil *Snap the Whip* (1872, Metropolitan Museum of Art).

[3] Peggy, an environmental enthusiast who became upset if a neighbor cut down a tree, would not have taken Church's drastic measures. Equally amusing were her painted enlivenments of the Ernst family home. As Prey recalls with some amusement, her mother also put her skills to practical use by creating a shuffleboard game and *trompe-l'oeil* flagstones in the basement, enlivened the kitchen floor with Jackson Pollock-style drip painting, and brightened a sunroom's walls with flowers and butterflies.

[4] Prey ultimately majored in German and the history of art.

[5] It was Faison who inspired Prey's interest in the development of southern German baroque and

rococo architecture and art; her honors thesis served as the first chapter of Faison's unfinished book on that subject.

6 *The Boston Globe*, Nov. 13, 2006, obituary of Lane Faison by Michael J. Bailey, Globe Staff. It might also be said that Prey is the perfect embodiment of Faison's lifelong advocacy for bringing artists ("people of the eye," as he called them) together with art historians ("people of the mind"). See John Hyland, Jr., appreciation of S. Lane Faison, Jr., in *CAA News* (March 2007), 30.

7 Prey remembers copying the folds of the remarkable dress in Ingres' portrait *Comtesse d'Haussonville* (1845, Frick Collection).

8 The Alliance for American Quilts, quoted on www.digitalheritage.org.

9 However, as Prey points out, in the late 1970s, Maine was far less populated with permanent residents and summer visitors—and artists—than it is in 2007.

10 Reproduced in Pamela J. Belanger, *Maine in America: American Art at the Farnsworth Art Museum* (Rockland, Maine: The Farnsworth Art Museum, 2000), 56.

11 See, for example, Cole's *Notch of the White Mountains (Crawford Notch)*, 1839, National Gallery of Art, Washington, D.C., reproduced in Earl A. Powell, *Thomas Cole* (New York: Harry N. Abrams, Inc., 1990), 95.

12 Doreen Bolger, David Park Curry, and H. Barbara Weinberg, with N. Mishoe Brennecke, *American Impressionism and Realism: The Painting of Modern Life, 1885-1915* (New York: The Metropolitan Museum of Art, 1994), 66.

13 Katie Zezima, "In Maine, Trying to Protect and Old Way of Life," *The New York Times*, March 25, 2007, Section 1, page 18, Column 1, discusses rising real estate values and the resulting vulnerability of Port Clyde's working docks, many of which are not owned by the fishermen who rely on them daily for their livelihoods.

14 Ben Neal, "Maine's Most Lucrative Lobster Zone Considers Limited Entry," *The Working Waterfront* [web edition], October 2003 and Nancy Griffin, "Port Clyde Joins List of 'Major' New England Fishing Ports," *The Working Waterfront* [web edition], December 2004.

15 Guy Pène du Bois, *Edward Hopper* (New York: Whitney Museum of American Art, c. 1931), as quoted in Belanger, *Maine in America*, 132.

[16] Among Hopper's Maine works are four watercolors done in Rockland, including *Haunted House* (1926); see Belanger, *Maine in America*, 132-135. A particularly notable Cape Cod painting is *Mrs. Scott's House* (1932), Maier Museum of Art, Randolph-Macon Woman's College, reproduced in Ellen M. Schall, John Wilmerding, and David M. Sokol, *American Art, American Vision: Paintings from a Century of Collecting* (Maier Museum of Art, Randolph-Macon Woman's College, 1990), 107.

[17] Charles Burchfield, "Edward Hopper, Classicist," in *Edward Hopper Retrospective Exhibition* (New York: The Museum of Modern Art, 1933), 16; quoted in Belanger, *Maine in America*, 132.

[18] Televised interview with the artist by Carol Lin, CNN Sunday, February 1, 2004.

[19] Paradoxically, these confined spaces apparently may contribute to respiratory ailments sometimes exhibited by the fishermen. Paint, chemicals, smoke from the burning of styrofoam buoys and rope ends, and bacteria growing on dry rope algae are just some of the toxins which, combined with dust and poor ventilation, have been linked to poor respiratory health in a study conducted by Vinalhaven's doctor and the Harvard School of Public Health. See Ben Neal, "In Lobstering, Not All the Hazards are at Sea," *The Working Waterfront* [web edition], March 2004.

Weblink to the Paris exhibition, *Barbara Ernst Prey: An American View* at the Mona Bismarck Foundation: http://www.synccityintl.com/mb/preyex.html

Weblink to interview with Barbara Ernst Prey and Sarah Cash: http://www.synccitytv.com/prey/prey1.html

Plates

NOCTURNE   2008, watercolor on paper, 21 x 28 inches

Barbara Ernst Prey

NOCTURNE II   2008, watercolor on paper, 21 x 28 inches

Barbara Ernst Prey

NOCTURNE V   2008, watercolor on paper, 21 x 28 inches

SANCTUM II   2007, watercolor on paper, 28 x 39 inches

WHITE WASH   2008, watercolor on paper, 20 x 29 inches

POINTS OF VIEW   2007, watercolor on paper, 27 x 39.5 inches

FATHER AND SON   2008, watercolor on paper, 20 x 28 inches

NOCTURNE III   2008, watercolor on paper, 28 x 40 inches

OWLS HEAD   2008, watercolor on paper, 27 x 39 inches

Barbara Ernst Prey

THE MEETING   2007, watercolor on paper, 21 x 28 inches

Barbara Ernst Prey

Wash Day   2008, watercolor on paper, 28 x 39.5 inches

ON EXHIBIT   2008, watercolor on paper, 27.5 x 21 inches

Barbara Ernst Prey

SELFLESS   2007, watercolor on paper, 20 x 28 inches

NOCTURNE IV   2008, watercolor on paper, 28 x 21 inches

Barbara Ernst Prey

PARADE ROUTE   2007, watercolor on paper, 21 x 27 inches

EXTENDED FAMILY   2007, watercolor on paper, 20 x 28 inches

PLACEHOLDERS   2007, watercolor on paper, 12 x 16 inches

WEATHERED WASH   2007, watercolor on paper, 28 x 40 inches

FLAG COLLECTION   2007, watercolor on paper, 16 x 11 inches

Barbara Ernst Prey

HEADING OUT   2007, watercolor on paper, 21 x 28 inches

FISHING GEAR   2007, watercolor on paper, 16 x 12 inches

SHROUDED   2006, watercolor on paper, 20 x 28 inches

Barbara Ernst Prey

LINE UP   2007, watercolor on paper, 20 x 28 inches

SILHOUETTES   2008, watercolor on paper, 24 x 38 inches

THE LONG HAUL   2004, watercolor on paper, 19 x 25 inches

BIOGRAPHICAL NOTES, COLLECTIONS & BIBLIOGRAPHY

1957	Born in New York City
1979	B.A., Williams College
1986	M.Div., Harvard Divinity School

Awards and Fellowships:

2004	New York State Senate Women of Distinction Award
1998	Artist in Residence, Westminster School, Simsbury, CT
1996	Best of Show, Westmoreland Museum of American Art
1986	Henry Luce Foundation Grant
1979	Fulbright Scholarship
1974	San Francisco Art Institute, Summer Grant

Listed:

Who's Who in the World
Who's Who in America, 50th Anniversary Edition
Who's Who of American Women
Who's Who in American Art

Selected Exhibitions:

2008	50 Years of NASA Art, Smithsonian Institution Traveling Exhibit
	An American View: Barbara Ernst Prey, Mona Bismarck Foundation, Paris
	Kennedy Space Center, NASA Commission
	United States Art in Embassies Program, U.S. Embassy, Paris, France
	United States Art in Embassies Program, U.S. Embassy, Madrid, Spain
	United States Art in Embassies Program, U.S. Embassy, Vilnius, Lithuania
2007	*Picturing Long Island*, The Heckscher Museum, Huntington, New York
	Kennedy Space Center, NASA Commission
	United States Art in Embassies Program, U.S. Embassy, Paris, France
	United States Art in Embassies Program, U.S. Embassy, Madrid, Spain
	United States Art in Embassies Program, U.S. Embassy, Vilnius, Lithuania
	Works on Water, Water Street Gallery, Seamen's Church Institute, New York
	From Port Clyde to Paris, Blue Water Fine Arts, Port Clyde, ME
2006	The White House
	United States Art in Embassies Program, U.S. Embassy, Paris, France
	United States Art in Embassies Program, U.S. Embassy, Madrid, Spain
	Kennedy Space Center, NASA Commission
	Chelsea Art Museum, New York, NY
	From Seacoast to Outer Space, The Williams Club, NY
	Guild Hall Museum, East Hampton, NY

Lift Off, Vanderbilt Planetarium, NY

Thirty Years of Painting Maine, Blue Water Fine Arts, Port Clyde, ME

2005 The White House

United States Art in Embassies Program, U.S. Embassy, Oslo, Norway

United States Art in Embassies Program, U.S. Embassy, Belarus

United States Art in Embassies Program, U.S. Embassy, Liberia

Kennedy Space Center, NASA Commission

Guild Hall Museum, East Hampton, NY

Works on Water, Blue Water Fine Arts, Port Clyde, ME

2004 The White House

United States Art in Embassies Program, U.S. Embassy, Oslo, Norway

United States Art in Embassies Program, U.S. Embassy, Belarus

United States Art in Embassies Program, U.S. Embassy, Liberia

Kennedy Space Center, NASA Commission

Observations, Harrison Gallery, Williamstown, MA

Guild Hall Museum, East Hampton, NY

Conversations, Blue Water Fine Arts, Port Clyde, ME

2003 The White House

An American Portrait, Arts Club of Washington D.C.

United States Art in Embassies Program, U.S. Embassy, Prague

United States Art in Embassies Program, U.S. Embassy, Oslo, Norway

United States Art in Embassies Program, U.S. Embassy, Belarus

United States Art in Embassies Program, U.S. Embassy, Liberia

2003 Kennedy Space Center, NASA Commission

The Valley Viewed: 150 Years of Artists Exploring Williamstown,
    Harrison Gallery, Williamstown, MA Curated by Katherine Carroll

Guild Hall Museum, East Hampton, NY

National Arts Club, NY

25 Years of Painting Maine, Blue Water Fine Arts, Port Clyde, ME

2002 United States Art in Embassies Program, U.S. Embassy, Prague

United States Art in Embassies Program, U.S. Embassy, Oslo, Norway

Obsession, Heckscher Museum of Art, Huntington, NY

American Art in Miniature, Gilcrease Museum, Tulsa, OK

Guild Hall Museum, East Hampton, NY

Patriot, Blue Water Fine Arts, Port Clyde, ME

A Trace in the Mind: An Artists Response to 9/11, Hutchins Gallery, C.W.
    Post College, Brookville, NY

2001 *Lightscapes*, Jensen Fine Arts, New York City

Guild Hall Museum, East Hampton, NY

American Art in Miniature, Gilcrease Museum, Tulsa, OK

Recent Watercolors, Blue Water Fine Arts, Port Clyde, ME

2000   *American Art in Miniature*, Gilcrease Museum, Tulsa, OK

1999   *Recent Watercolors*, Jensen Fine Arts, New York City

Heckscher Museum, Huntington, NY

American Art in Miniature, Gilcrease Museum, Tulsa, OK

Guild Hall Museum, East Hampton, NY

1998   *American Art in Miniature*, Gilcrease Museum, OK

Express Yourself, Portland Museum of Art, ME

1997   Museum of the Southwest, Midland, TX

Recent Acquisitions, Farnsworth Museum of Art, Rockland, ME

1996   The Westmoreland Museum of American Art, Awarded *Best in Show*

1995   The Philadelphia Museum of Art

1994   Farnsworth Museum of Art Benefit Auction Exhibit, Rockland, ME

1993   Blair Art Museum, Hollidaysburg, PA

Johnstown Art Museum, Johnstown, PA

1989   *Women's Art*, Williams College, Williamstown, MA

1988   Museum of Fine Arts, Nassau County, NY

1986   Harvard University, Cambridge, MA

Selected Collections:

The Brooklyn Museum

The Smithsonian American Art Museum

Orlando Bloom

President and Mrs. George Bush

President and Mrs. George W. Bush

The White House

The Farnsworth Art Museum

Williams College

Williams College Museum of Art

The Taiwan Museum of Art

Mellon Hall, Harvard Business School

The Henry Luce Foundation

Reader's Digest Corporation

Prince and Princess Castell

Prince and Princess Johannes Lobkowicz

Prince and Princess Michael Salm

Mrs. C. Robert Allen

Mr. Herbert Allen

Mr. and Mrs. James Broadhurst

Mr. Sam Bronfman

Mr. and Mrs. Barrett Brown

Mr. and Mrs. Duncan Brown

Mr. and Mrs. Russell Byers Jr.

Governor Hugh Carey

Mr. and Mrs. Nathan Clark

Mr. and Mrs. Chris Davis

Mr. and Mrs. Boomer Esiason

Mr. and Mrs. Allan Fulkerson

Senator and Mrs. Judd Gregg

Mr. and Mrs. Edward L. Hennessy

Mr. Franklin Kelly

Mrs. Henry Luce III

Mr. and Mrs. Dan Lufkin

Mr. and Mrs. James McCarl

Mr. Richard P. Mellon

Mr. Roger Milliken

Dr. and Mrs. Frank Oakley

Ambassador and Mrs. John Ong

Mr. Peter O'Neill

Mr. and Mrs. Howard Phipps, Jr.

Ambassador and Mrs. Mitchell Reiss

Ambassador and Mrs. Craig Stapleton

Dr. and Mrs. James Watson

Mr. and Mrs. Jimmy Webb

Selected Bibliography and Interviews:

Varia, Transatlantica: Review d'etudes americaines (American studies Journal), Sorbonne, Paris
April, 2008 (interview)

Where a Painter Travels for a Visual Feast, More Magazine, May, 2008

Time Off – Museum Exhibitions Europe: An American View: Barbara Ernst Prey, The Wall Street Journal,
December 2, 2007 (Paris selection)

An American in Paris, Women's Wear Daily, October 26, 2007

Out and About, Fine Art Connoisseur, December, 2007

An American View: Barbara Ernst Prey, essay by Corcoran Museum of Art Curator Sarah Cash

An American View: Barbara Ernst Prey, Paris Capitale, November, 2007

Barbara Ernst Prey – An American View, BeauxArts, November, 2007, January, 2008

Le Maine en Aquarelles, Version Femina Paris, November 18, 2007

Vision Americaine, Artistes Magazine, January/February, 2008

An American View, Maisons Cote Ouest, December/January, 2008

Paris: Barbara Ernst Prey, Azart, November/December, 2007

Fausse Tranquillite, Le Journal de la Maison, December, 2007

Aquarelles d'Amerique, Mon Jardin & Ma Maison, December, 2007

An American View, Pariscope, October 18, 2007; December, 2007

Barbara Ernst Prey, Détente Jardin, January/February, 2008

An American View, L'Ami des Jardins et de la Maison, January, 2008

Dazzled from Port Clyde to Paris, USA Today Magazine, July, 2007, p. 38-43, Cover

A Breath of Fresh Air: Painting Nature Now, Fine Art Connoisseur, October, 2007

Brush with History, Houston Chronicle Zest Magazine, April 15, 2007, Patty Reinert

Prey at Home and Across the Pond, Maine Sunday Telegram, August 12, 2007

Bill Moyers, PBS, April 27, 2007

Nature in an Untouched State, The New York Times, February 18, 2007

Visions of Long Island, Newsday, February 1, 2007

High Art, Harvard Magazine, November/December, 2006

So Watery, the Works of Barbara Ernst Prey, The New York Sun, October 25, 2006

Time Off - Exhibit: Works on Water, The Wall Street Journal, October 19, 2006

Barbara Ernst Prey in New York, PBS WLIW, October, 2006 (interview)

The Critic's Choice, The New York Daily News, October, 2006

1010 Wins Radio New York with Joe Montone, October, 2006 (interview)

Barbara Ernst Prey: Reflections, essay by Paul Lieberman, Los Angeles Times Cultural Writer, 2006

Museums, The Washington Post, December 16, 2005

Barbara Ernst Prey: Works on Water, essay by Corcoran Gallery of Art Curator Sarah Cash, 2005

Names and Faces: An Artist Ready for Liftoff, The Washington Post, July 22, 2005 (interview)

The Difference in Barbara Ernst Prey, Maine Sunday Telegram, August 28, 2005 (interview)

NPR, July 2005 (interview)

An Artist on a Space Mission, Newsday, July 17, 2005 (interview)

Footlights: Artist Shooting for the Stars, The New York Times, July 10, 2005. (interview)

Capturing the Moment, Florida Today, July 13, 2005 (interview)

On the Town, The New York Sun, April 15-17, 2005

2005 Women of Distinction, Distinction Magazine, March 2005 (interview)

Barbara Ernst Prey: Studio Visit, PBS WLIW- NY, January 2005

Painter Seeing a Bigger Picture, Los Angeles Times, October 4, 2004

Prey Exhibit in Maine, Coastal Living Magazine, Summer 2004

Columbia Tribute, CNN News with Carol Lin, February 2, 2004 (interview)

Columbia Tribute, CNN Newssource, February 1, 2004 (interview)

NPR, February 2004 (interview)

The Fine Art of the Space Age, The Washington Post, January 26, 2004

Artist Reaches New Heights, The Boston Globe, January 20, 2004 .

Tribute Reflects the Lives of Columbia Crew, Newsday, February 1, 2004

Artist Fulfills New Mission for NASA, AP Newswire, January 26, 2004

1010 Wins Radio New York with Joe Montone, February 1, 2004 (interview)

WOR The Ed Walsh Show, February 1, 2004 (interview)

Prey's Columbia Tribute, CBS News Radio, February 1, 2004 (interview)

White House Artist, Voice of America, December 4, 2004 (interview)

Talk of the Town, The New Yorker, December 1, 2003

She Answered a Call from Washington, The New York Times, December 21, 2003

CNN, Paula Zahn NOW, December 23, 2003 (interview)

Larry King Live, CNN, December 2003 (interview)

HGTV White House Christmas Special, December, 2003 (interview)

End Page: Barbara Ernst Prey, The Robb Report, August 2003, September 2003

Arts and Antiques Magazine, Summer 2003

A Trace in the Mind: An Artists Response to 9/11, catalog essay by Charles Riley, C.W. Post University

Public Lives, The New York Times, October 31, 2002

Williamstown Artist Compared to Homer, The Paper, November 29, 2002

On the Loose in New York, The International Art Newspaper, April 2001

Famous Last Words, Linda Stasi, The New York Post, April 22, 2001

The Critic's Choice, The New York Daily News, April 2001

The Joan Hamburg Show, April 2001 (interview)

True North: Barbara Ernst Prey Inspirations, Maine PBS, 2001 (interview)

Watercolor 2001: Barbara Ernst Prey New Work, American Artist Magazine 2001

Where Artists Live Their Work Comes Alive, Newsday, Annual Home Magazine Issue, Cover

PBS-Channel 21, The Metro Report, New York, June 1999 (interview)

The Critic's Choice, The New York Daily News, January 1999

Art Market: Prey Exhibit, The International Art Newspaper, January 1999

WOR-AM The Joan Hamburg Show (interview)
The Exchange with Channel 12, January 1999 (interview)
The Maine Focus: Barbara Ernst Prey, Interview with Andrew Bowser, WERU, October 7, 1997
Winners, Newsday, November 1996.
Career Moves: Two Successful Artists Offer Advice, American Artist Magazine, Watercolor 1991
Taiwan Pictured Through Western Eyes, Asia Magazine, July 1987
U.S. Painter Views Taiwan With Color and Contrast, China Post, May 1987

Artwork Commissions:
NASA Commission – 2005 Shuttle Relaunch
NASA Commission – 2005 The x-43
NASA Commission – 2005 International Space Station Print
NASA Commission – 2004 Columbia Commemorative
NASA Commission – 2004 International Space Station
White House Christmas Card, 2003

Lectures:
The National Gallery of Art, "The Watercolors of Winslow Homer"
U.S. Embassy, Oslo, "Business Supporting the Arts"
U.S. Embassy, Prague, "The 9/11 Series"
U.S. Embassy, Paris
U.S. Embassy, Madrid
Thyssen-Bornemisza Museum, Madrid

Selected U.S. Embassy and Consulate Collections:

Abu Dhabi	Lima
Athens	Madrid
Baghdad	Managua
Bogata	Marseilles
Brasilia	Mexico City
Buenos Aires	Nassau
Cairo	Panama
Caracas	Rangoon
Guatamala	Seoul
La Paz	Tunis

Website: www.BarbaraPrey.com